WHERE DOES MY FOOD COME FROM?

Published in 2022 by Welbeck Children's Books Limited
An imprint of the Welbeck Publishing Group
Based in London and Sydney.
www.welbeckpublishing.com

Design and layout © Welbeck Children's Limited 2022
Text copyright © Annabel Karmel
Illustration copyright © Alex Willmore

Annabel Karmel has asserted her moral right to be identified as the author of this Work in accordance with the Copyright Designs and Patents Act 1988.

Author: Annabel Karmel
Illustrator: Alex Willmore
Co-writer: Stella Caldwell
Photography: Ant Duncan
Food stylist: Holly Cowgill

Props stylist: Tamsin Weston
Design Manager: Matt Drew
Editorial Director: Joff Brown
Production: Melanie Robertson

ISBN 978 1 78312 912 6

Printed in Dongguan, China
10 9 8 7 6 5 4 3 2 1

FSC
www.fsc.org
MIX
Paper from responsible sources
FSC® C144853

My Sticker Chart

Color in the star or add your own sticker to each recipe and craft activity when you've tried it!

 Eggs

 Cheese

 Tomatoes

 Pasta

 Strawberries

 Honey

 Chocolate

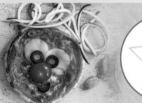

WHERE DOES MY FOOD COME FROM?

ANNABEL KARMEL

With Fun, Easy Annabel Karmel Recipes!

Annabel Karmel

WELBECK

Alex Willmore

Hello my foodie friend!

I spy a budding chef in the making! But when you're munching on your favorite foods, do you ever wonder how they reached your plate?

This book is a jam-packed trail of food discovery, filled with crafty activities, fun experiments, and yummy recipes you'll love to make. Plus, I let you in on a host of weird and wacky foodie facts to wow your friends and family.

Like my kids, ketchup might be your sauce of choice, but do you know how many tomatoes it takes to fill a ketchup bottle?

And next time you slurp up your spaghetti, picture this: before clever machinery was invented, pasta makers used their feet to mix and knead the dough!

I'll even let you in on how to tell when an egg is super fresh or past its best—how eggsellent is that?

Foodie maestro, it's time to get exploring!

Contents

Eggs

You can eat goose eggs, duck eggs, and even fish eggs. But I'm the most popular egg—I come from a chicken!

1. Only female chickens, called hens, lay eggs. Egg farmers keep hundreds of hens on large farms and feed them grain.

2. Each hen lays around one egg a day in a nesting box. The eggs roll onto a moving belt, where workers carefully pack the eggs into trays.

3. A special machine checks the eggs for cracks, to make sure they're good enough to eat. Then each egg is stamped with a date, to show how fresh it is.

4. The eggs are sorted by size and packed into boxes. Now they are ready to be taken to the store—and onto your breakfast table!

5. Eggs are full of goodness. You can boil them, fry them, or scramble them. And they're an important ingredient in everything from cakes to custard!

Medium

Large

If I lie flat on the bottom of a bowl of water, I'm super fresh. If I sit on one end, I'm OK to eat. But if I float, I'm past my best!

Fresh

OK to eat

Time to throw away!

8

Multicolored Eggs

Make remarkable rainbow eggs—it's super simple!

You will need:

- Several hard-boiled eggs
- Kitchen or craft gloves
- Paper towels
- Bottles of food coloring
- Spray water bottle
- Small rubber bands

1. Put each egg in the center of a paper towel. Bunch the paper around the egg, twist the end tightly, and tie it with a rubber band.

2. Put your gloves on and hold the egg in one hand. Use your other hand to squeeze out a few drops from each food coloring bottle onto the paper covering. Leave some empty space between the drops on the paper.

3. Spray small amounts of water into the center of each color patch, until the paper is completely colored.

4. Gently press the paper to get rid of any extra water. Then leave the covered eggs in the fridge to dry overnight.

5. When the eggs are dry, unwrap your beautiful creations!

Ask an adult to boil me before you paint me. And make sure I've cooled down before you start!

It's easier to make these in a silicone muffin tin—then they're easier to remove.

Eggs-tra Special Frittata Muffins

PREPARATION: 10 mins   COOKING: 40 mins

Ingredients

5 oz new potatoes
5 medium or large eggs
1.5 oz Cheddar cheese, grated
4 spring onions, chopped
2 oz frozen peas
6 cherry tomatoes, chopped
Sunflower oil for greasing

1. Pre-heat the oven to 400° F. Grease a 12-hole muffin tin with oil.

2. Cook the new potatoes in boiling water for 12 to 15 minutes. Drain, cool and cut into ½ inch cubes.

3. Beat the eggs in a large bowl. Stir in the potatoes, cheese, spring onions, peas, and tomatoes. Pour the mixture into the muffin tin.

4. Bake for 20 to 25 minutes until well risen and golden. Leave to cool for a few minutes, then release from the muffin tin and cool on a wire rack.

Veggie Makes 12

Beary Tasty Bear Pancakes

PREPARATION: 15 mins   COOKING: 20 mins

Ingredients

1 cup self-raising flour
1 tsp baking soda
Pinch of salt (for babies over 1)
¼ cup superfine sugar
1 medium or large egg, beaten
1 ½ tbsp butter, melted
1 cup milk
125g Ricotta cheese

DECORATION

Blueberries
Edible eye decorations
Black writing icing

Veggie

Makes 4 bears

1. Measure the flour, baking soda, salt, and sugar into a bowl. Mix in the egg, butter, milk, and Ricotta together in a jug.

2. Add the wet ingredients and whisk together until smooth.

3. Heat a little sunflower oil in a frying pan. Add spoonfuls of mixture to the pan. Fry for 2 minutes on each side until golden and cooked through.

4. To make a bear, make a large oval pancake for the body and a round pancake for the head. Make 4 small round pancakes for feet and ears. Make 2 oval pancakes for the arms. Decorate with blueberries and edible eyes, and make a mouth and paws with the black icing pen.

Cheese

There are so many different types of cheese, from hard to creamy, crumbly to stinky. But we all start off as the same thing: milk!

1. It all begins with dairy cows on a farm. They munch lots of grass in order to make plenty of milk. They make so much that a farmer milks them twice a day with a special machine.

2. A tanker collects the milk from the farm and takes it to the cheese factory.

3. Workers heat the milk in a vat. They add rennet, which contains good bacteria and enzymes. It helps the milk to turn into cheese!

4. Workers cut the curds into smaller pieces and add salt. They press them into molds to make wheels of cheese, like the ones in supermarkets.

5. Now the workers store the cheese in a cool place until it is ripe. Some kinds of cheese are ripe in a few weeks. Others need a few months or even years to ripen!

DID YOU KNOW?

You might think that mice like cheese… but in fact, they prefer peanut butter!

6. There are all sorts of ways to eat cheese. You can sprinkle it over a baked potato, melt it on a tasty pizza, or use it to make a delicious, gooey sauce. What's your favorite cheesy treat?

Cheesy Robots

Use cubes of cheese to make these cute little bots!

You will need:
- Toothpicks*
- Firm cheese, such as Cheddar cheese
- Pretzel sticks
- Raisins
- Grapes or olives

1. Cut the cheese into cubes to make the robot bodies. Cut some smaller cubes for their heads.

2. Arrange two cubes of cheese on a plate to make a robot's body and head.

3. Stick pretzel sticks into the sides of the body to make arms.

4. Press raisins into the head to make a face, and into the body to make buttons.

5. You can make legs by pressing two toothpicks through the bottom of the body. Fix grapes or olives to either side of the toothpicks.

6. Repeat these steps to make a robot family!

Did you know you can make cheese from the milk of sheep, goats, yaks, reindeer, llamas, camels ... and even donkeys!

*Grown-ups, please supervise children with toothpicks!

Strawesome Cheese Wands

PREPARATION: 15 mins   COOKING: 18 mins

Ingredients

13.2 oz ready-rolled puff pastry
1 egg, beaten
1 cup Mozzarella cheese, grated
⅓ cup Parmesan cheese, grated

OPTIONAL
Poppy seeds
Sesame seeds

Veggie   Makes 24

1. Pre-heat the oven to 400° F.

2. Line a large baking sheet with non-stick baking paper.

3. Unroll the pastry and roll out to make a slightly thinner rectangle. Brush the sheet with the beaten egg. Sprinkle half of the cheeses over one half of the sheet. Fold over the pastry and re-roll back to the original shape, so the cheeses are in the middle. Brush with more egg and sprinkle over the remaining cheeses on top.

4. Divide the pastry in half lengthways. Slice each half into 12 strips to make 24 strips in total. Using your fingers, twist each strip to make a straw. Place on the baking sheet.

5. If you like, you could sprinkle them with poppy seeds, sesame seeds, or some extra grated cheese.

6. Bake for about 15–18 minutes until golden and crisp.

This has been my most popular recipe on Instagram and everyone loves it. You can cut the mixture into any shape—why not try circles or hearts?

Cheesy Carrot Super Stars

PREPARATION: 10 mins   COOKING: 15 mins

Ingredients

7 oz carrots, peeled and grated

⅓ cup Cheddar cheese, grated

2 tbsp Parmesan, grated

2 medium or large eggs, beaten

4 tbsp self-raising flour

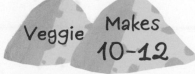
Veggie   Makes 10–12

1. Pre-heat the oven to 400° F.

2. Put the carrots into a clean towel, and squeeze out as much liquid as possible.

3. Place in a bowl. Add the cheeses, eggs, and flour (plus seasoning if the stars are for babies over one year old).

4. Line a baking sheet with non-stick baking paper. Put a star cutter onto the sheet. Fill the cutter with the carrot mixture. Press down firmly. Remove the cutter and repeat. You could also use a small round cutter instead of a star.

5. Bake in the oven for about 15 minutes until set and lightly golden.

Tomatoes

It's great to be a tomato! We're squishy, nutritious, and delicious. It all starts with just a tiny tomato seed...

1. Tomato growers plant rows of seeds in a greenhouse. They water them every day until their tiny green shoots start to grow upward.

DID YOU KNOW?

The Spanish town of Bunol holds a festival where more than 40,000 people throw over 150,000 tomatoes at each other!

2. The plants start to grow tall and strong. Yellow flowers bloom and get fertilized by the bees buzzing around their petals. The flowers drop to reveal tiny green tomatoes.

3. The little tomatoes gradually grow in size. They turn from green...to orange...to bright red. Pickers pluck the ripe tomatoes from the plants and pack them into crates.

4. Workers load the crates of tomatoes onto trucks to be weighed, sorted, and packed.

DID YOU KNOW?

How many tomatoes do you think are in a bottle of ketchup? It's 25!

5. Finally, those little tomatoes make it to the store for you—in all sorts of types and colors!

Not all tomatoes are red. We can also be green, orange, or purple. We can be pear-shaped, egg-shaped, and heart-shaped, too!

6. Tomatoes are so versatile. You can chop them, squish them, or mix them into yummy things like tomato juice and tomato ketchup.

20

Grow Your Own Tomatoes

Planting and growing tomatoes is fun and easy!

You will need:
A packet of cherry tomato seeds
Potting soil
Small pots (such as clean yogurt cups)
Larger pots, about 12 inches wide

1. Fill the small pots with potting soil, almost to the top. Drop two seeds into each pot, then sprinkle a layer of soil over the seeds.

2. Put the pots on a sunny windowsill. Keep the soil moist, but don't let it get too wet.

3. After five to ten days, the seedlings will start to sprout. When they are about 2.5 inches high, carefully plant them in larger pots outside. Place them in a sunny spot.

4. Water the plants every day. The first tomatoes should be ready to eat after about four weeks.

We tomatoes hate the cold and love the sun! Sow our seeds in early April, and only plant the seedlings outside when there is no more frost.

Zingy Tomato Pasta

PREPARATION: 10 mins   COOKING: 20 mins

Ingredients
8 large ripe tomatoes
2 tbsp tomato purée
2 tbsp olive oil
1 onion, finely chopped
2 cloves garlic, crushed
⅓ cup water
knob of butter
pinch of sugar
2 tbsp basil, chopped
1 ½ cups uncooked penne pasta

1. Blanch the tomatoes in boiling water for 30 seconds. Drain and cool in cold water. Peel the skins away and de-seed the tomatoes. Chop them roughly.

2. Heat the olive oil in a saucepan. Add the onion and garlic, and fry for 5 minutes.

3. Add the tomatoes, purée, and water. Cover with a lid and simmer for 15 minutes. Add the butter, sugar, and basil.

4. Cook the pasta in boiling water according to the packet instructions, then drain and add to the sauce. Toss together and serve with grated cheese.

Veggie   Serves 4

Mini Pizza People

PREPARATION: 15 mins   COOKING: 20 mins

Ingredients

13.2 oz ready rolled puff pastry
⅓ cup tomato purée
1 clove garlic, crushed
2 tbsp sun-dried tomato paste
5 oz cherry tomatoes, sliced
2 tbsp basil, chopped
¾ cup Mozzarella cheese, grated
Olives, Cheddar cheese, and
veggies for decoration

Veggie   Makes 4 pizzas

1. Pre-heat the oven to 425° F.

2. Unroll the pastry and cut out 4 x 4-inch circles. Place them on a baking sheet lined with baking paper. Prick the base with a fork.

3. Mix the tomato purée, garlic, and the sun-dried tomato paste together in a bowl. Spread over the bases. Top with the cherry tomatoes, the basil, and the cheese.

4. Bake in the oven for 15-20 minutes until the tops are golden brown and the bases are crisp.

5. Now decorate with olives, Cheddar cheese, and veggies to make super silly faces!

Pasta

We can be long, short, flat, or squiggly. Some of us look like seashells and others like bowties! Have you ever wondered what we're made of?

1. Pasta is made from durum wheat. A farmer plants the wheat in a warm country such as Italy. The wheat turns golden under the sun, and a combine harvester collects the grain.

2. Special machines in a mill grind the grain into a fine flour called semolina. Then a truck takes the semolina to a pasta factory.

3. Workers mix the semolina with water to make a squishy dough. Then they put the dough through a mold to make the pasta. Different molds cut different pasta shapes.

4. The soft, wet pasta is hung up to dry. It takes several hours.

DID YOU KNOW?

Before machinery, pasta was kneaded by foot.

25

5. The dry pasta is now ready to be packed and boxed. Then it travels by ship and truck around the world. That's how it gets into stores...into your saucepan...and into your favorite pasta meal!

6. Eating pasta is a good way to give your body energy. You can mix it with a tasty sauce, stir it into soup, or bake a delicious cheesy pasta dish in the oven.

How do you tell if your spaghetti is overcooked? Throw it at the wall and it's likely to stick! The more pasta cooks, the gummier it gets! (But don't throw ME, please!)

Pasta Mosaic

Press pasta into clay to make a fabulous fish,
a pretty flower, or a beautiful butterfly!

You will need:

A selection of small pasta shapes
Liquid hand sanitizer
Food coloring bottles
Large, sealable food bags
Newspaper
Play dough or air-drying clay

1. Half-fill the plastic food bags with pasta shapes.

2. Take the first bag and add a few squirts of hand sanitizer,
   and several squirts of a food color. Seal the bag.

3. Jumble the bag with your hands until all the pasta is colored.

4. Repeat with the other bags of pasta, using different colors for each one.

5. After 15 minutes, lay the pasta out on a sheet of newspaper. Wait for it to dry.

6. To make the mosaic, place some play dough or clay on a sheet of newspaper.
   Roll it out to about ½ inch thick, and cut it into a tile.

7. Press the colored pasta into the play dough or clay to make your design.

8. If you're using clay, leave it to dry for the amount of time indicated on the
   packaging. Now your mosaic will be preserved forever!

27

Easy Pea-sy Fusilli

PREPARATION: 5 mins   COOKING: 15 mins

Ingredients

5 cups uncooked fusilli pasta
2 oz peas
5 ½ oz smoked bacon, chopped
⅔ cup crème fraîche
¼ cup Parmesan cheese, grated
3.5 oz cherry tomatoes, halved

1. Cook the pasta in boiling water according to the packet instructions. Add the peas a few minutes before draining.

2. Fry the bacon in a frying pan until crispy. Add the crème fraîche and bring up to the boil.

3. Add the pasta and peas, tomatoes, and Parmesan. Toss together and serve at once.

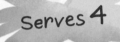

Serves 4

TIP!
Make a vegetarian version by replacing the bacon with 3.5 oz of small broccoli florets. Add these to the pasta 4 to 5 minutes before the end of the cooking time.

Bowl You Over Spaghetti Bolognese

PREPARATION: 10 mins   COOKING: 40 mins

Ingredients

1 tbsp olive oil

1 large onion, finely chopped

1 carrot, peeled and finely chopped

1/2 red pepper, deseeded and finely diced

1 clove garlic, crushed

9 oz lean ground beef

1 x 14.5 oz can chopped tomatoes

1 heaped tbsp tomato purée

2 tsp fresh thyme, chopped or 1/2 tsp dried thyme

1. Heat the olive oil in a saucepan. Add the onion, carrot, and pepper. Fry over the heat for 5 minutes.

2. Add the garlic and beef and brown with the vegetables.

3. Add the tomatoes, tomato purée, and thyme.

4. Simmer covered with a lid for 30 minutes.

5. Serve with spaghetti.

Serves 4

Strawberries

We strawberries are delicious to eat and lovely to look at too. But did you ever wonder how we get onto your table?

1. Farm workers plant baby strawberry plants in a field. They sit on the back of a big tractor to do it!

DID YOU KNOW?
The strawberry isn't a true berry! On the other hand, avocadoes and bananas ARE actually berries!

2. The workers build a plastic greenhouse, called a polytunnel, around the strawberries. The polytunnel gives the growing strawberries lots of light and protects them from hungry birds.

3. White flowers bloom, and bees and ladybug buzz around the petals. As the petals fall away, little green strawberries grow in their place.

4. The green strawberries become plump and red. Then workers pick the juicy fruit and pack it into crates.

5. Workers weigh, check, and pack the strawberries. They keep the fruit cool so it doesn't turn bad. Then a truck takes the packed strawberries to stores.

6. Strawberries are delicious to eat all on their own! Or you can turn strawberries into sweet treats like smoothies, cheesecakes, and strawberry jam.

I'm not just a tasty treat—I'm good for you too! Strawberries are packed full of vitamin C, and I'm a natural teeth cleaner for your pearly whites.

Strawberry Snake

This sneaky snake, made with slithers of strawberry and banana, is a party table pleasssss-er!

You will need:
6 strawberries
One banana, peeled
Natural yogurt
2 raisins, a chopped blueberry, or 2 chocolate chips

1. Ask a grown-up to cut the banana and five of the strawberries into slices. Arrange them in a snakey shape, mixing the banana and strawberry slices in a pattern.

2. To make the head, place a whole strawberry on the end of the snake.

3. Ask a grown-up to make a small cut in the strawberry for the mouth, then slice a little bit of strawberry or banana to make a tongue.

4. To make the eyes, add two small blobs of yogurt to the head and top with raisins, blueberries, or chocolate chips.

Mini Strawberry Cheeky Cheesecakes

PREPARATION: 1 hr   COOKING: 5 mins

Ingredients

3 oz graham cookies

3 tbsp butter

¾ cup cream cheese

½ cup double cream

1 tsp vanilla extract

¼ cup icing sugar

9 oz strawberries, sliced into small pieces

Veggie   Makes 4

1. Put the cookies into a zip lock bag. Finely crush using a rolling pin.

2. Melt the butter in a saucepan. Add the cookies to the pan, and coat them well with the butter.

3. Spoon the mixture into 4 x 3-inch round rings. Press down firmly and chill in the fridge for 20 minutes.

4. Mix the cream cheese, cream, vanilla, and icing sugar together in a bowl.

5. Spoon on top of the cookie base. Arrange the chopped strawberries on top.

6. Chill for 30 minutes, then serve.

"Simply the Best" Parfaits

PREPARATION: 10 mins   COOKING: 25 mins

Ingredients

⅔ cup double cream
¾ cup Greek yogurt
12 oz strawberries
2 oz meringues, broken

Veggie

Makes 4

1. Blend 4 oz of the strawberries until smooth, using a stick blender.

2. Chop the remaining strawberries.

3. Whip the double cream, then stir in the Greek yogurt and meringues.

4. Spoon half of the cream mixture into 4 small bowls or glasses.

5. Pour over the strawberry coulis and half of the strawberries. Spoon the remaining cream mixture on top, and top with the strawberries.

Honey

You probably know that I'm made by bees. But where do these buzzybodies get what they need to make such a sticky treat?

1. Worker bees fly from flower to flower. Their use their long tongues like straws to suck up a sweet juice, called nectar. In their tummies, the nectar turns into runny honey.

2. The bees fly back to their hive and spit the runny honey into the spaces of a honeycomb. Other bees beat their wings to help make it thicker. Then they seal the honeycomb with wax.

DID YOU KNOW?
It takes 5,000 bees to make just one jar of honey!

3. A beekeeper removes the wax and takes a small amount of honey from each hive. The honey is put into large drums, and a truck takes it to a factory.

4. At the factory, the honey is cleaned with special machines. Then it's placed in large vats that keep it at the right temperature.

DID YOU KNOW?
Honey bees can fly at 15 miles per hour—as fast as a charging bull!

5. The honey is put into jars. It's all set to be sent to stores, ready to be spread on your toast. Yummy!

6. Honey is packed full of vitamins and other good things. You can use it instead of sugar to sweeten things. Drizzle it over pancakes, mix it into natural yogurt, or stir it into a hot drink. Delicious!

Bee Drinking Pool

Making honey is thirsty work! But bees can't swim, and can get into trouble drinking from deep water. Make them a safe place for a drink in your garden.

You will need:
A shallow dish
Stones, pebbles, or shells
Marbles or glass stones

1. Find a place near flowers to place your dish. Fill it with stones, pebbles, or shells. These will make "islands" for the bees to stand on.

2. Add marbles and glass stones if you have them. These will make your water station look pretty in the sunlight.

3. Pour water over the stones and marbles, but make sure you don't completely cover them.

4. Check your bee water station every day. It might get too full if it rains, or it might dry up in hot weather.

As well as making honey like me, bees help pollinate plants which grow into the food that we eat!

You're My Honey, Challah

PREPARATION: 3 hrs   COOKING: 30 mins

Ingredients

5 cups strong white bread flour

2 ¼ tsp fast action dried yeast

1 ½ tbsp superfine sugar

2 medium or large eggs, beaten

1 tsp salt

3 tbsp runny honey

6 tbsp butter, melted

⅔ cup warm water

3 oz raisins, roughly chopped

TO GLAZE

1 egg, beaten

4 tbsp sesame seeds

2 tbsp runny honey

Veggie

Makes 2 loaves

1. Measure the flour, yeast, sugar, and salt into a large bowl. Mix the eggs, honey, butter, and water together in a jug.

2. Pour the wet ingredients into the bowl and mix well. Tip out onto a work surface and knead into a soft dough for 10 minutes. Place in an oiled bowl. Cover with clingfilm and leave to rise for 2 1/2 hours.

3. Pre-heat the oven to 410° F. and line a large baking sheet with baking paper.

4. Tip the dough onto the work surface. Knock the bread back for a few minutes, then knead in the raisins. Divide the dough into two. Divide each half into three and roll out to three long pieces about 16 inches long. Braid the pieces together, then tuck the end underneath. Repeat with the remaining half.

5. Place both loaves on the baking sheet. Cover loosely with clingfilm and leave to prove for 30 minutes, or until doubled in size.

6. Brush the bread with beaten egg and sprinkle with sesame seeds. Bake for 25-30 minutes until golden. Brush the top with honey. Leave to cool on a wire rack.

Stickylicious Honey Chicken Kebabs

PREPARATION: 40 mins   COOKING: 6 mins

Ingredients

¼ cup runny honey

1 tbsp soy sauce

1 1/2 tbsp rice wine vinegar

2 cloves garlic, crushed

2 chicken breasts, sliced into cubes

1 red pepper, sliced into pieces

1 tbsp sunflower oil

Makes
4

1. Measure the honey, soy sauce, vinegar, and garlic into a bowl. Add the chicken pieces and leave to marinate for 30 minutes.

2. Soak 6 wooden kebab skewers in water. Thread the chicken and pepper onto the skewers.

3. Heat the oil in a large frying pan. Add the kebabs and fry for 5-6 minutes on both sides until golden, and the chicken is cooked through.

Chocolate

It's great being as scrumptious as me! But did you know I started off as a bean?

1. Farmers in countries like Ghana in Africa, or Brazil in South America, grow cocoa trees. Tiny flowers on the trees turn into plump pods that grow as big as footballs. Workers pick the pods when they are ripe.

2. Cocoa beans are inside the pods. Workers cut open the pods, take out the beans, and lay them out in the sun to dry.

3. The beans are sent to factories around the world. There they are cleaned, roasted, and ground into a thick, brown paste. The paste is mixed with milk and sugar.

4. Next, the paste is squished and squashed by a huge roller. Then the mixture is heated and cooled in huge tanks until it becomes smooth and creamy.

43

5. The chocolatey mixture is poured into molds and made into bars. Then they are cooled, wrapped, and packed. The chocolate is ready to be sent to stores—and ready to melt in your mouth!

DID YOU KNOW?
M&Ms were made for US soldiers in World War II. Their hard candy shells meant they could be kept in their pockets without melting!

6. Chocolate can be made into all kinds of sweet treats. It's used in cake, ice cream, and desserts, and it makes a delicious drink as hot chocolate.

The main ingredient in milk and dark chocolate is cocoa solids. But white chocolate is made from a different part of the cocoa bean, called cocoa butter. That's why some people say I'm not "real" chocolate! Huh!

44

Chocolate Lollipop Gifts

These sweet treats will make perfect gifts for your friends and family—as long as you don't eat them yourself!

You will need:

3.5 oz milk, dark,
or white chocolate, chopped
Popsicle sticks
A baking tray
Baking paper
A heatproof bowl
A dessert spoon

TOPPING SUGGESTIONS:

Sprinkles, silver balls, nuts, raisins, mini marshmallows, jellybeans

1. Line a baking tray with baking paper.

2. Ask an adult to help you melt the chocolate. You can put it in a heatproof bowl over a pan of simmering water, or you can microwave it on full power for 15 seconds at a time, until it is melted.

3. Put 1 tablespoon of chocolate on the lined baking tray. Use the back of a dessert spoon to shape it into a circle. Then lay one end of a lollipop stick on top, and make sure it is covered in chocolate. Repeat with the rest of the chocolate.

4. Design your lollipops while the chocolate is still wet. Try some funky designs!

5. Put the lollipops in the fridge to harden for 20 minutes.

Owl Always Love You Cupcakes

PREPARATION: 30 mins   COOKING: 25 mins

Ingredients

FOR THE CUPCAKE

1 ⅛ cup self-raising flour
¼ cup cocoa powder
1 stick butter, softened
½ cup superfine sugar
2 medium or large eggs
2 oz chocolate chips

Makes 12

FOR THE FROSTING

1 cup icing sugar
1 stick salted butter, softened
3 oz plain chocolate, melted

TO DECORATE

Oreo cookies
Brown and orange M&Ms

1. Pre-heat the oven to 350° F. Line a 12 hole muffin tin with cupcake papers.

2. Measure all of the cupcake ingredients into a bowl (except the chocolate chips). Whisk together with an electric hand whisk. Stir in the chocolate chips, then spoon into the papers.

3. Bake in the oven for 20-25 minutes until well risen. Leave to cool on a wire rack.

4. Whisk the butter and icing sugar together in a mixing bowl. Add the the chocolate and whisk until well mixed.

5. Spread the frosting over the cakes.

6. Slice the Oreo cookies in half. Place two cut sides on top of the cupcake to make the owl's eyes. Stick two brown M&Ms on top for the eyeballs. Slice one half of a cookie in half to make the eyebrows, and add to the top of the cake. Add an orange M&M for the nose. Repeat with the remaining cakes.

Choc Chip Little Monster Cookies

PREPARATION: 10 mins   COOKING: 25 mins

Makes
28

Ingredients

¾ cup butter, softened
⅔ cup soft brown sugar
¼ cup superfine sugar
1 egg, beaten
2 tsp vanilla extract
2 cups plain flour
2 tsp cornstarch
1 tsp baking powder
1/2 tsp salt
8 oz plain chocolate chips
White fondant
Black fondant
White icing

1. Pre-heat the oven to 400° F.

2. Line two baking sheets with baking paper.

3. Measure the butter and sugars into a bowl. Whisk until fluffy using an electric hand whisk. Add the egg and vanilla. Whisk again. Add the remaining ingredients and whisk until the mixture has come together.

4. Chill for 15 minutes.

5. Roll into 28 balls. Place on the baking sheets and press down. Bake for 15 minutes until pale golden. Leave to cool on a wire rack.

6. Once cold, make eyes and a mouth out of the fondant. Add to the cookies to make a monster's face!

About
Annabel Karmel

ANNABEL KARMEL

With expertise spanning more than 30 years, London-born mother of three Annabel Karmel reigns as a bestselling international author, the UK's no. 1 children's cookery author, and a world-leading expert on devising delicious, nutritious meals for babies, children, and families.

Since launching her revolutionary cookbook for babies—*The Complete Baby and Toddler Meal Planner* in 1991—a feeding "bible," which has become the second bestselling nonfiction hardback of all time, Annabel has cooked up 47 cookbooks and raised millions of families on her recipes.

Annabel's vision has always been to ensure every child gets the nutrients they need for their development and long-term health, and her unique, healthy recipe combinations and advice have made her a true pioneer in her field. A powerhouse among parents, Annabel's trusty cookbooks can be found in family kitchens all over the world.

Annabel also connects with 1.5 million families on a weekly basis via her website and social media community. And most parents will have Annabel's #1 rated recipe app safely installed on their smart phones for on-the-go inspiration.

From kitchen table to global stage, Annabel uses her revolutionary food expertise and experience to campaign for better food standards. In 2006, Annabel received an MBE in the Queen's Birthday Honours for her outstanding work in the field of child nutrition, and she is also well recognized as a leading female entrepreneur and "mompreneur," spending time mentoring other parent-run businesses.